Cherry Blossom Friends

A suggestion on how to read this book.
This is a book about the incredible gift of the cherry trees
to America from Japan, and all the wonderful gifts that trees
bring, including fresh air and the animals that might live around
the blossoming trees in Washington, D.C.
As you will see, it is designed to be read to a wide range of
listeners. Each page has two distinct sections:
the "Rhyme and Riddle" and the "Did you know...."
It is suggested to first read the "Rhyme and Riddle" section from
cover to cover. Then read the "Did you know..." sections.
These interesting facts do not need to be read in sequence.

Cherry
Blossom
Friends

Words and Pictures by
Corkey Hay DeSimone

2nd Edition Copyright 2009
Gentle Giraffe Press
Printed in Hong Kong

Have you heard about the
3,020 famous flowering trees,
that blossom each spring in the
Washington breeze?

They were given as a gift
to Washington from Tokyo, Japan.
Yes, the Americans and Japanese had a plan.
They would plant these pretty pink trees all in a row,
as a reminder that friendship can blossom and grow.

Can you guess what trees they might be?
Turn the page and you will see.

The Japanese Cherry Trees

To celebrate this gift each spring
a special lantern is lit,
and the flame burns bright.
It is such a beautiful sight.

This lantern sits beside the Tidal Basin,
among the cherry trees.
Another great gift of friendship
from the Japanese.

What special lantern could this be?
Turn the page and you will see.

Did you know...
In 1912, the same year that the Titanic sailed, 3,020 cherry trees were given as a
gift from one capital city to another – Tokyo to Washington, D.C.
Have you ever had to carry a plant home from the garden store? Did you handle
it with care? So how did the Japanese and Americans get 3,020 trees from
Tokyo to Washington? First, in Japan, they were carefully loaded onto a
ship to cross the Pacific Ocean. They arrived in Seattle, on the west coast
of America, but still had a long way to go. So they were placed
in a cooled freight train, which crossed more than 2,500
miles from the west coast to the east coast.
From Japan, the journey took 40 days.
What an incredible trip.

The Japanese Stone Lantern

What other gifts do the cherry trees bring?
They can be a place for animals to frolic in the spring.

These beautiful blossoming cherry trees
might be a home to butterflies, birds and bees.
A place for raccoons to climb and foxes to hide,
for squirrels to run, jump and glide,
for blue herons to perch and robins to nest,
for skunks to sleep or take a rest,
for turtles to sun on a log sunken halfway,
for bald eagles to soar, swoop and play.

Many animals may enjoy the gift of trees from Japan.
Turn the page to name as many animals as you can.

Did you know...
The Stone Lantern that sits beside the Tidal Basin is eight feet tall, over 350 years
old and has a twin in Japan. The lantern has not always sat surrounded by cherry
trees in Washington, D.C. It once stood outside an ancient temple in Japan,
where its twin lantern still stands to this day. In 1954, Japan presented the Stone
Lantern to America as a gift celebrating 100 years of friendship. Sadly, it was not
100 years of perfect peace. In 1941, Japan and America went to war.
After four years it came to an end, and it was time to mend the wounds of war.
The Stone Lantern is an important symbol of renewed friendship and peace.
It is lit every spring in a beautiful ceremony during the
National Cherry Blossom Festival.

Are you ready? Listen please,
for your first riddle about an animal
that may live among the cherry trees.

I nest in the cherry blossoms
of Washington, D.C.
I am a small bird,
can you find me?

Just like the cherry blossoms,
I'm a sign of spring.
I sit in the cherry trees
and sing, sing, sing.

I have dark gray wings
and an orange chest.
I lay blue eggs in my nest.

Take a guess, what can I be?
Turn the page and you will see!

Robin

I swim under the cherry blossoms
of Washington, D.C.
I am a reptile, can you find me?

I live in water, but lay eggs on land,
I dig my nest in soft soil and sand.
On the Potomac River is where I dwell.
I have a long neck and a protective shell.

Take a guess, what can I be?
Turn the page and you will see.

Did you know...
The Washington Monument is the tallest building in Washington, D.C.
It is a monument to George Washington and it took a very long time to
build. During the Civil War its construction stopped because the
builders ran out of money. For close to 24 years it stood unfinished in the
middle of the National Mall and was about 150 feet tall. Look closely
and you will see that the color of its stone is two-tone. Some say that the
bottom is a different color because during construction it was
exposed to many years of dust and dirt. Others say that when
construction began again, marble from the original quarry was no longer
available, so they had to use a different colored stone. What we
do know is that when finished in 1884, it stood just over 555 feet tall
and it was the tallest building in the world.

In 1965, the Japanese made another generous gift of 3,800 cherry trees
to First Lady, Lady Bird Johnson, wife of President Lyndon Johnson.
This time, the trees were grown in America. Many of these trees were
planted on the grounds of the Washington Monument. It is such a
beautiful sight to see the Washington Monument rising above
the blossoming trees.

Turtle

I climb among the cherry blossoms
of Washington, D.C.
I love acorns, can you find me?

I run up the trunks
and scurry around the trees.
I leap from branch to branch
with incredible ease.

Take a guess, what can I be?
Turn the page and you will see.

Did you know...
The Japanese cherry trees were planted more than 26 years before
the Jefferson Memorial was built. To make room for the new memorial some
cherry trees needed to be moved. Since the cherry trees were
beloved, this made many people unhappy. A group of women protested
and promised to chain themselves to the trees, so the trees wouldn't be cut
down. In the end, a deal was made and it was promised that new trees would
be planted to replace any lost trees. Today, it is hard to imagine the cherry
blossoms without the Jefferson Memorial. Thomas Jefferson was our
third president and a great and smart man, who wanted a country that
was free, where everyone had the right to learn and enjoy liberty.

Squirrel

I soar above the cherry blossoms
of Washington, D.C.
I'm a symbol of
America and liberty.
I'm a bird of prey
can you find me?

I have bright yellow eyes,
talons and a hooked beak.
I have a white-feathered head
and my call is a shriek.

Take a guess, what can I be?
Turn the page and you will see.

Did you know...
George Washington helped pick the site of the new capital city and laid the
U.S. Capitol building cornerstone. However, the nation's capital wasn't always in
Washington, D.C. The government met in many different cities, and finally in 1800, the
Congress, the Supreme Court and the Library of Congress moved into the new
Capitol. Sadly, during the War of 1812, the British set the building ablaze. If not
for heavy rains, the fire might have burned for days. This did not stop the Americans.
When the war ended the Capitol was rebuilt and has continued to change and grow.

More than 100 years after the Capitol was built, the Japanese cherry trees were
planted on the grounds. If only George Washington were here to see how beautiful his
Capitol grounds would be, painted in pink during the blossoming of the cherry trees!

Bald Eagle

I fish beneath the cherry blossoms
of Washington, D.C.
I'm a large wading bird,
can you find me?

I have a long neck and up to a 6 foot wing span.
I love to eat small fish whenever I can.
On my long legs, I hunt by standing still in one place.
I fly along the Tidal Basin with incredible grace.

Take a guess, what can I be?
Turn the page and you will see.

Did you know...
Ben Franklin wanted the wild turkey to be the national bird of America.
However, in 1782, the founding fathers made the bald eagle the emblem of the
United States and it has become a strong symbol of America's freedoms.

Almost 200 years later, the bald eagle almost became extinct. Hunting and
the use of a pesticide (a poisonous chemical used to kill bugs) that thinned the
shells of the eagles' eggs were at fault. Since the eagles were not able to lay
healthy eggs, they had very few chicks. The bald eagle was declared an
endangered species, eagle hunting was outlawed and the use of this particular
pesticide was stopped. The American bald eagle bounced back!
Now you can see bald eagles flying over the cherry blossoms
of D.C. and along the Potomac River, healthy and free.

Blue Heron

I hide among the cherry blossoms
of Washington, D.C.
I'm smart and sly,
can you find me?

I am part of the dog family, but not a pet.
I'm a wild animal, but not a threat.
I have black-tipped ears
and a long bushy tail.
You can spot my furry
red coat without fail.

Take a guess, what can I be?
Turn the page and you will see.

Did you know...
In 1914, about two years after the cherry trees arrived, the first stone of the Lincoln Memorial was set. The Lincoln Memorial has 36 columns around the outside, one for each of the 36 states in America the year Lincoln died. During his presidency the country was divided. There were 11 Confederate states that wanted to leave the Union. The 11 southern Confederate states fought the 25 northern Union states during the Civil War. Lincoln worked to keep the United States one country.

As you walk around the memorial you can see two bands of states engraved above the columns. On the lower band are the 36 Civil War states. On the upper band are the names of the 48 states that were part of America when the memorial was finished. Look closely and you may find your state. Are you from Alaska or Hawaii? These states were added later; a marker can be found outside the memorial. Also inside is the statue of Lincoln sitting deep in thought. It is 19 feet tall and weighs 350,000 pounds. President Lincoln was our 16th president. He ended slavery and reunited the country. Yes, Lincoln was a man of courage!

Red Fox

I can graze among the cherry blossoms
of Washington, D.C.
I find cherry leaves tasty,
can you find me?

My father is a buck and my mother is a doe.
I walk on hooves, I have no toes.
My tail has a white underside
which I flash when alarmed,
if I think I might be chased,
hunted or harmed.

Take a guess, what can I be?
Turn the page and you will see.

Did you know...
The Smithsonian Castle is the oldest building on the National Mall.
How it came to be is an amazing story. James Smithson was from England and had
never set foot in America. However, when he died in 1829, he gave his life savings to
the United States and no one knows for certain why. His fortune was sent on a ship to
America in 11 boxes containing gold coins. It safely arrived and was melted down and
made into American gold coins that were worth over half a million dollars.
James Smithson had asked that the money be used to set up the Smithsonian
where people could share all the things that they learned and discovered.
At last count there were nineteen museums, and 9 research sites.
His gift grows and blossoms just as the cherry trees do.

Whitetail
Deer

I live among the cherry blossoms
of Washington, D.C.
I'm black and white, what can I be?

You can smell me coming a mile away.
Don't get too close or else I'll spray!

Take a guess, what can I be?
Turn the page and you will see.

Did you know...
The White House is where the American President works and lives, but it was never George Washington's office or home. In 1800, President John Adams was the first to live in the White House.

During the War of 1812, the British set the White House on fire. It was thought that it was first painted white to cover the burn marks. More accurately, it was painted white because it was built with sandstone. The paint helps protect this soft and porous stone from cracking in the wet and cold winters.

When First Lady Helen Taft lived in the White House, she worked closely with the Japanese to bring cherry trees to Washington. On March 27, 1912, First Lady Helen Taft and Viscountess Chinda, wife of the Japanese Ambassador to the United States, planted the first two cherry trees. Those two trees sit at the edge of the Tidal Basin with a historic marker at their base.

Skunk

I climb in the cherry blossoms
of Washington, D.C.
I come out at night,
can you find me?

In the spring I can have
six babies, but usually three.
I can make my den in a hollow tree.
I have a masked face and a ringed tail.
Watch for me and my babies on the trail.

Take a guess, what can I be?
Turn the page and you will see.

Did you know...
In 1958, the Japanese Pagoda that sits by the Tidal Basin was another generous
gift from Japan. Like a puzzle, it arrived in many pieces, without building instructions.
It came in five big crates, is made of stone and weighed 3,800 pounds. It was not easy
to put together and staff from the Library of Congress were recruited to help.

What is a pagoda? It is a multistory Buddhist tower, built as a memorial or shrine.
Buddhism is one of the religions practiced in Japan.

In Japan, to show the balance of nature, gardens include water, stone and plants.
The Japanese Stone Pagoda sits beneath the cherry trees, at the side of the
Tidal Basin, perfectly mixing the three important Japanese elements of
water, stone, and plants in harmony.

Raccoon

I buzz around the cherry blossoms
of Washington, D.C.
I'm an important insect,
can you find me?

One of my jobs
is to pollinate plants.
Other plant pollinators are
butterflies, beetles and ants.

I sip and gather nectar
from flower to flower.
With it, I can make honey
and it gives me power.

Take a guess, what can I be?
Turn the page and you will see.

Did you know...

The Smithsonian Carousel that twirls and whirls around has 57 carved wooden jumping horses, one menagerie animal, two chariots, one spinning tub and one special dragon. It was originally built in 1947 by the famous carousel maker, The Allan Herschell Company. They made more than 3,000 carousels, many of which were used by traveling carnivals. The Smithsonian Carousel was first in a park in Baltimore before it was moved onto the National Mall in 1975 and placed close to the Smithsonian Castle. You can ride this carousel every day but Christmas Day. After you take a ride stroll through the Hirshhorn Museum Sculpture Garden where in the spring, you can enjoy blossoming cherry trees.

Bees

I stroll among the cherry blossoms
of Washington, D.C.
I love to picnic, what can I be?

I'm the only animal that can plant a tree,
and save land for wildlife to roam free.

Take a guess, what can I be?
Turn the page and you will see.

Did you know...
The trees that were gifted in 1912 were not the first cherry trees given to America
from Japan. An original group of 2,000 trees took the long trip from Japan and
arrived in January 1910. Sadly, after being inspected by a team from the
Department of Agriculture they found the trees to be infested with insects and
disease. To protect American growers it was decided that the trees must be burned.
President and First Lady Taft were very disappointed, as was the mayor of Tokyo.
The Japanese and Americans did not give up and in March 1912,
the 3,020 famous flowering trees arrived in our capital city.

When you receive a gift it is important to give in return,
and Japan and America have a long history of giving.
In 1982 it was America's turn again. A flood destroyed the Yoshino
cherry trees in Japan. The Japanese horticulturalists came with a plan
to take cuttings from the Washington cherry trees,
so they could grow and replace the trees that were lost to the flood.

You and me!

Did the Japanese and Americans foresee
all the good things that come with a tree?
Like all the animals that frolic, eat and live,
and the fresh clean air that the trees give.

There is no better gift that you can give
to the earth, your city or the place you live.
So plant at least one tree each and every spring,
and prepare to be amazed by the gifts it will bring.

Did you know...
It is estimated that about 3,700 cherry trees are still growing in
Washington, D.C. Over 6,800 trees have been thoughtfully
given to Washington by Japan. The cherry trees remind us of
the great friendship between America and Japan, and that all
friendships need attention and care. We must not take friendship
for granted. We must share, be fair, and always remember that
good, strong friendships are extremely rare.

About the Author and Illustrator

Corkey Hay DeSimone lives with her
family close to Washington, D.C.
She was the founding owner, designer
and illustrator for Corkey's Kids,
a children's clothing company.
In 2003, after 12 years,
she sold Corkey's Kids so that she could
turn her focus to writing and illustrating
educational children's books.

After selling Corkey's Kids,
she renamed her company
Gentle Giraffe Press.
She has since written, illustrated
and published 22 books
and several more are in the works.

Books by
Corkey Hay DeSimone

The Planet Hue

Mammal Animal Board Book
First Edition
Mammal Animal Activity Book
First Edition

Air and Space Board Book
Air and Space Activity Book

Sports Legends Board Book
Sports Legends Activity Book

Panda Promise Hardbound Book
Panda Promise Board Book
Panda Promise Activity Book

Dinosaur Explore Board Book
Dinosaur Explore Activity Book

Mammal Animal Board Book
Second Edition
Mammal Animal Activity Book
Second Edition

Desert Dwellers Board Book
Desert Dwellers Activity Book
Desert Crawlers Board Book
Desert Crawlers Activity Book

Butterfly Friends
Butterfly Friends Board Book
Butterfly Friends Coloring Book